Safe at Home

Written by Michèle Dufresne

PIONEER VALLEY EDUCATIONAL PRESS, INC.

Animals live in many kinds
of homes. Some make nests.
Some dig holes.
Some live in shells.
Homes help keep animals safe.

Animals need homes to protect themselves from bad weather and predators. Animal homes are also good places to store food and care for animal babies.

A den makes a good home
for animals. A den can be a cave
or a hole. Animals go
into their dens to **doze**.

A den helps animals
cope with the **cold**.

Some animals line their dens with grass
or fur to make them warm and soft.

Many animals have nests.

Nests make good homes for **birds**.

Birds make nests
from grass and twigs.

Nests keep bird eggs safe.

Some birds build their nests
high to keep eggs safe from
snakes and other animals.

Hives make good homes for **bees.**

Lots and lots of bees live in a hive.

Hives keep bees
and their eggs safe.

A hive has one queen bee and many worker bees and drone bees.

This is a mole.

Its home is a **burrow**.

The mole pokes up

from the burrow to see

if it is safe to come out.

A burrow is like a tunnel in the ground.
One mole can live in tunnels that cover
more than two acres.

Some animals have shells
for homes.

They take their homes with them!

A turtle's shell is part of its body.
Some turtles can pull their heads
and legs into their shells.

This is a crab.

The crab lives in a shell.

When the crab walks,

so does its home!

Hermit crabs do not make their own shells—they find empty ones to live in. When hermit crabs outgrow their shells, they find new ones.

glossary

animals:
living things
that move,
eat, and grow

bees:
insects that
live in hives
and make
honey

birds:
animals with
feathers and
wings; most
can fly

burrow:
a hole or
tunnel in the
ground where
animals live

cold:
a low
temperature
that can be
uncomfortable

doze:
to sleep lightly
or rest